RECIPES

for

ROMANCE

50 Ways to Sweeten Your Love Life

by Leslie & Jimmy Caplan

New World Library
Novato, California

New World Library
14 Pamaron Way • Novato, CA 94949

© 1996 Leslie and Jimmy Caplan

Cover photo: Thea Schrack
Cover and text design: Nita Ybarra

Library of Congress Cataloging-in-Publication Data
Caplan, Leslie, 1953 -
Recipes for romance : 50 ways to sweeten your love life
by Leslie and Jimmy Caplan.
p. cm. ISBN 1-880032-78-3 (alk. paper)
1. Man-woman relationships. 2. Sexual excitement. 3. Love.
4. Intimacy (Psychology) I. Caplan, Jimmy, 1949- . II. Title.
HQ801.C276 1996

306.7—dc20   95-35700
                                                        CIP

Distributed by Publishers Group West
10 9 8 7 6 5 4 3 2 1
Printed in Canada

To our children
David and Kelly Leigh —

When we grow up
we want to be just like you.

CONTENTS

INTRODUCTION

Nothing satisfies the soul like being in love. We crave romantic love so much that we vicariously seek it out in literature, music, and theater. Unfortunately, our own love experiences are often lackluster by comparison.

When we first fall in love, everything is great. Love takes off like a fireball soaring into the night sky. It makes us feel so wonderfully alive that we expect it to ascend forever. But when that fireball starts falling to earth, our hopes and expectations of what love should be sometimes fall as well.

We prepared *Recipes for Romance* to help bridge the gap between where you are now and the heights you want to reach. Currently you may question why your love relationship doesn't sparkle the way it used to, and long for the days when your partner could set your soul on fire. You may even wonder why everyone else seems to be having all the fun. If you are feeling any of these things, take heart; you are not alone.

What we have learned from many happy couples and from our own experiences is that falling in love and staying in love are more a matter of *being* the right person than just *finding* the right person. And there really is a simple formula for becoming that person: Demonstrate your love and appreciation for your partner *each and every day*. The affection you express by finding new ways to say "I love you" will not only make your partner feel sublime, but also unlock the door to more exhilaration than you ever thought possible!

Be adventurous and creative. Don't be afraid to try the recipes in this book because you feel they "just aren't you." Start with some of the simpler ones, then move on to those requiring more time and planning. Chances are, once you get off the back burner, your partner will be more stimulated and responsive than he or she has ever been!

We wish for you a romantic life, filled with the joy and pleasure that accompany it. By following these recipes, you are taking the initiative to reignite the fireball of love and get it rolling again.

Bon appétit!

Some Enchanted Evening

Too much of a good thing can be wonderful.

~Mae West

1. DATE NIGHT

One of the best and most often-ignored ways of keeping your relationship novel and exciting.

- 1 night alone each week
- 2 large helpings of creativity
- Receptivity to change
- Willingness to take turns

Choose one night each week that belongs to the two of you and no one else. To avoid falling into the "dinner-movie-home-to-bed" syndrome, take turns planning the date. Be creative. Try some of the ideas listed in this book and originate some of your own.

Here's what makes it work. You must be open to each other's invitation and accept willingly — even if it's something you would not normally do or even want to do. Date Night will give you the opportunity to get to know new things about each other.

Practice Date Night regularly and you will have many surprises along the way. Friends of ours married for twelve years started Date Night and the husband soon found he was enjoying the evenings his wife planned more than his own.

Sample Serving

Another couple we know has had what they call an "affair" almost every Wednesday afternoon during their thirty-five years of marriage. Their memories are better than most people's dreams and demonstrate the cumulative value of Date Night. One of their favorite affairs took place some years ago when they reserved a room at one of the first hotels in Los Angeles to feature waterbeds. Their children heard about their plans and sent them off on their voyage with a sailor's cap and a giant safety pin.

2. A NIGHT ON THE TOWN

Adventure is the champagne of life. ~G. K. Chesterton

- 1 uncommon means of transportation
- 1 dozen flowers
- 2-3 of your partner's favorite treats
- Propensity to pamper
- Day spa visit (optional)

Show up in a rented limousine or horse-drawn carriage as a delicious surprise in itself or as part of an evening's event. In addition to flowers and a loving smile, have your partner's favorite candies, magazines, or other treats in view as he or she steps inside.

As a prelude to this or any other night on the town, treat your partner to a manicure, pedicure, facial, or body massage. Hire a professional or do it yourself. Many cities now have day spas that offer all these services under one roof. Any one or a combination of these pleasures will be welcome whether your partner is a regular or newcomer to pampering.

3. STRANGERS IN THE NIGHT

Love is what makes a crowd disappear
when you're with someone. ~Elvis Presley

- 1 place with unfamiliar faces
- Provocative attire
- Desire to role play
- No expectations

Have you ever thought about picking up your partner? That's right, meeting your one true love again for the first time.

This works best when you dress up independently of one another. If you're living in the same house, perhaps one of you can prepare for the evening elsewhere. For your rendezvous, choose a place where singles meet and where it is unlikely you will run into any of your friends. It could be a bar, dance, or social event. Come separately but at approximately the same time, circulate, and see what happens.

Picking up your partner once or twice a year is a great way to revive the joy of dating and show renewed interest in your partner. No two nights will be the same if you leave your expectations at home.

Sample Serving

Leslie is shy about meeting new people, and one evening I enjoyed sitting across from her at a bar and watching her deal with overtures from other men. We started to make eye contact, so I asked the bartender what she was drinking and ordered her another glass of wine. I actually felt nervous as I walked over to her a few minutes later, introduced myself, and asked to join her. We began conversing as though we were meeting for the first time, and then continued with an intimate evening of dinner and dancing. We romanced each other until 3:30 in the morning!

4. CHEZ SHANGRI-LA

Feast on each other and your love will feed on itself.

- Exotic food
- Ethnic costume
- Romantic music
- Pleasing environment

Turn your home into the hottest dining spot in town. Start with your own menu or order a meal for two from a caterer or restaurant specializing in exotic foods. Add the appropriate dress, music, and ambiance to draw out the full flavor. Allow this concoction to simmer for an hour or two and your partner will really be salivating.

Sample Serving

A friend of ours is a sensational gourmet cook. One evening her boyfriend walked through the front door and was transported instantly to Italy. He was captivated by the smell of garlic, the music of Pavarotti, the look of his girlfriend wearing a Roman toga, and the newly transformed dining room table, decorated like the Italian flag. The meal of pasta and Italian delicacies could not have tasted more authentic. And as if this weren't enough of "La Dolce Vita," she served the final course of gelato and cappuccino on the floor in front of the fire.

"The only drawback to Italian food," her boyfriend noted, "is that three or four days later, you're hungry again."

JUST THE TWO OF US

To love and be loved is to feel the sun from both sides.

~David Viscott

5. DEVOTED TO YOU

Your partner's wish is thy command.

- Generous amount of time reserved only for your partner
- Unconditional surrender
- Butler or maid costume (optional)

Devote yourself to your partner's needs for an entire day, or even part of a day, and see if you rediscover what most couples confess: Yes, it is more fulfilling to give than to receive.

It begins by announcing to your partner that you will be his or her servant for the next ___ hours. (The first time, you may want to try it for only one or two hours.) You are now available to do exactly what he or she wants and grant every wish that is within your power. It might include running errands or doing household chores, baby-sitting the kids, cooking a meal, washing the car, polishing shoes, giving a massage, writing a love poem, or fulfilling one of your partner's sexual fantasies.

This is a terrific way to communicate that your partner is definitely number one in your life. For an added effect, consider renting a butler or maid outfit from a costume shop.

6. DYNAMIC DUO

Familiar acts are beautiful through love. ~P.B. Shelley

- 1 outstretched hand
- Desire to whistle while you work
- Ability to render service with a smile

Offer to help your partner do some chores that he or she usually does alone: Cook a meal, do the housework or gardening, buy groceries, pick up the kids. It can turn a mundane job into something romantic.

Sample Serving

An entrepreneur who travels often on business has always packed his own bags. One evening his wife helped him so that he could avoid doing it at the last minute. Her help made things so much easier that he now looks forward to her assistance before every trip. And her special touch of leaving a love note or gift (cologne, a new mystery novel, etc.) carefully tucked away in a crevice of the suitcase continually takes him by surprise. The simple act of packing together gives this couple a little more time together before business trips, and this successful businessman even admits that his wife's sense of style helps him make a greater impact at meetings.

7. EASY LISTENING

Indulge in the sweet sound of your partner's voice,
and vice versa.

- 1 book or musical instrument
- A little time in a quiet space

Set aside ten minutes toward the end of each day (about an hour each week) to read to each other: short stories, inspirational quotes or passages, poetry. Or serenade your partner with some songs on the guitar or piano.

Hearing the sound of your partner's voice is a refreshing alternative to late-night talk shows.

Sample Serving

Jimmy and I like to go to the bookstore together and pick out books that interest us both. We particularly enjoy reading in bed at night and while traveling. Periodically we pause to share stimulating ideas, or read sentences or paragraphs to each other. It's like reading two books at the same time.

8. HE SAID, SHE SAID

*At the touch of love
everyone becomes a poet.* ~Plato

- 1 secluded setting
- Writing materials
- Artful brainstorming
- Skillful collaboration

Create or find an area inside or outside your home where you and your partner will be undisturbed. Choose a subject that interests you both and select a medium to express your creativity on that subject. You can write alternate lines of poetry, compose the music and lyrics of a song, co-author a screenplay, start a travel journal as a reminder of your trips together, or develop fifty recipes of your own to please each other.

This can be done on a one-time or regular basis. Either way, your collaboration could result in something as simple as a greeting in a birthday card, or as involved as a published manuscript.

9. LAZY DAY

This is the day to let it all veg-out!

- 12 or more hours
- Freedom from distractions
- Responsiveness to your heart instead of the clock

Pick a day when your only commitment is to have fun with each other. Take care of all important errands beforehand. Don't answer the telephone on Lazy Day or you will end up responding to other people's needs. The password throughout the day is spontaneity; the only question you need to ask yourselves is, "What do we really want to do right now?"

Sample Serving

We convinced a dear couple we know to try Lazy Day, and they didn't even get out of bed until 3:00 p.m.! They said it felt great — no pangs of guilt or fatigue from rushing. They were still going strong when they went to see a midnight movie. What they enjoyed most was the freedom from pressure while they ran around town, and the joy in just allowing the day to unfold. They had fun collecting small mementos to remind them of their Lazy Day.

10. WALK AND TALK

Steal your partner away for the pause that refreshes.

- 2 pairs of walking shoes or sneakers
- Active listening
- Warm clothing (as needed)
- Eagerness to communicate feelings

Regular walks provide one of the easiest ways to maintain strong and frequent communication in a relationship. It's as easy as putting one foot in front of the other for at least twenty to thirty minutes. "I'm too busy" is no excuse.

Don't let the elements deter you. A walk in the rain or falling snow can be as romantic as a stroll beneath a full moon. You can vary it by driving to a different neighborhood or hiking trail you've never experienced and start from there. One important rule: No cellular phones or pagers!

Sample Serving

A friend of ours is an ordained minister in New Jersey. He advises the couples he marries to take a walk together every day. He and his wife have rigorously followed that advice during their sixteen-year marriage and call it the secret to their success as a couple. For them, the walk creates a relaxed setting to share or vent "stuff" that might not get out otherwise; they find it far superior — and so may you — to sitting and talking at home where distractions occur. And even if there's nothing in particular to relate, it's a great way to exercise and take in some fresh air. You can do it no matter what kind of shape you're in!

SPECIAL DELIVERIES

Sometimes the littlest thing makes the biggest difference.

11. P.S. I Love You

Anything that is written to please a loved one is treasured.
~Rick Eisenberg

- 1 stockpile of stationery, cards, and Post-it™ notes
- Ample supply of decorative pens
- Banner, sign, or billboard (optional)
- 1 rhyming dictionary (optional)
- Attitude of gratitude

Always have a stack of blank notes and cards ready so you can send a note to your partner whenever the mood hits you. And if lightning doesn't strike, do it anyhow at least once each week. Mark Twain wrote his wife a love letter every day, and they lived in the same house!

A short note expressing gratitude for last night's date or your partner's concern for your career or feelings is an excellent way to communicate how much you value your relationship. It shows that even in the midst of your busy day, you are thinking about the one who matters the most. If you want to be dramatic and show off your message, create a banner, special order a message from a sign company, or rent a billboard.

Many women feel that their men rarely think about them when they are at work or away from the house. Men, show them they are wrong!

Sample Serving

I'll never forget peeking out the window one Valentine's Day and seeing the shocked look on Jimmy's face when he arrived home. Stretched across the front of the house was a ten-foot, hot pink laminated banner announcing to him and the entire neighborhood, "Leslie loves Jimmy." Once inside the house, he followed a trail of notes and his favorite chocolate bars leading him to the bedroom door. Lounging on the bed in my tiara and diaphanous hot pink nightie, I was waiting for my Prince Charming.

12. X Marks the Spot

The adult version of hide-and-seek.

- 1 or more cards, 1 pad Post-it™ notes
- 1 pen or pencil
- 1 roll Scotch tape
- 1 cassette tape and recorder (optional)

Write a note or card and place it in an unusual place but where your partner can't miss it: inside the washing machine or tool box, on the car steering wheel or visor, inside a shoe, purse, or briefcase. Post-it™ notes are fun to put all over the house.

A variation of this idea is to record a message on a cassette tape and put it in your partner's Walkman, stereo, or car tape deck.

Sample Serving

A practical joker once left a romantic card taped to the underside of the toilet seat cover. (Imagine her boyfriend's surprise when he attended to nature's call!) Instead of thanking her, he acted as though nothing unusual had happened. She grew more and more curious, until finally she ran to the bathroom and lifted the seat cover, only to find that her card had been replaced by one from him. They tell us that it has been difficult to surpass that note exchange!

13. EXTRA! EXTRA!

Your partner will definitely want to read all about it.

- Ad copy
- Knowledge of your partner's preferred reading material

Put a classified ad in the section of a newsletter, newspaper, or magazine that your partner reads regularly. It can acknowledge his or her unique qualities, refer to a tender moment in the relationship, or propose a tryst.

An alternative is to tape or insert a note in your partner's reading material where it is likely to be seen. For computer couples, e-mail love notes can add a soft touch to a high-tech day.

14. GOING PUBLIC

It's better if they're watching.

- 1 hot beverage in a special mug
- Pastry, snacks, reading materials (optional)
- 1 card with flowers
- Lunch with tablecloth and candles
- Willingness to find your partner with an audience

Surprise your partner at work during a morning or afternoon break with gourmet coffee or tea served in a commuter or personalized photo mug. This simple offering will be remembered long beyond your visit and can be expanded to include a favorite pastry, snacks, or reading materials.

Men, don't be so private with your flowers. Send them to a place where other people can admire them with her (work, a luncheon with the ladies, etc.) and tell her how lucky she is! Or surprise her by leaving flowers in areas where she would not normally expect them, like on the hood of her car.

Ladies, instead of taking your man out to lunch, try bringing a homemade lunch or catered meal to where he works. Whip out a table-cloth and candles and join him; or give him a long kiss (see recipe 21), tell him you're sorry you can't stay, and rush off. Either way you will certainly get him salivating, and other eyes turning.

15. VALUE-ADDED BOUQUET

The fragrance goes so much further.

- 1 bouquet of fresh-cut flowers
- 1 related or unrelated gift
- Bountiful imagination

Double the pleasure of flowers by adding something extra to the bouquet. It can be a vase, cutting shears, flower-pressing kit, seeds, or an unrelated gift such as homemade cookies or tickets to the theater.

Many men also enjoy receiving flowers, particularly when they are part of a larger gift idea. If your man doesn't, substitute with a bouquet of balloons. The number of successful combinations are limited only by your sense of imagination.

Jimmy buys me fresh flowers almost every week, yet I am still surprised by the creativity behind many of the arrangements. My favorite was a pastel blend of flowers in a beautiful vase, with $20 bills spread throughout. At the top of the bouquet was a postcard from a dating service I had joined years before. Written over the message that someone wanted to meet me were the words "TAKEN FOR GOOD."

16. FAMILY TIES

They'll love to hear the good news.

- 1 note or card
- 1 pen
- Address of your partner's parents
- 1 gift or flowers (optional)

Send a note of appreciation about your partner to his or her parents. "Thank you for creating such a wonderful person. He/she has brought so much joy into my life." Consider including a small gift or flowers.

17. TIME CAPSULE

We store preserves so that sweet fruit may always be in season.

- 1 memory basket
- Artifacts of love
- Desire to keep on giving

Give your partner a special box or container to keep all the love memorabilia you send or share (such as cards, notes, pictures, concert ticket stubs). It can be purchased at a store, or you may want to exercise your artistic talents and make one out of glass, metal, or wood.

An inscription on the inside — even something as simple as "From (your initials) to (his or her initials)" — can be intimately beautiful and remind your partner of your devotion whenever the time capsule is opened.

18. A STAR IS BORN

Be your own agent and strut your own ego.

- Guts
- 1 8-by-10 glossy photo
- 1 permanent marker or pen
- 1 quality frame
- Glamour or boudoir photographer (optional)

For no apparent reason, send a handsomely framed 8-by-10 inch glossy photograph of yourself to your partner. Sign it with something like, "To my biggest fan, I love you forever."

If you want to add the professional touch, consider glamour or boudoir photography. A glamour photographer works with a hair stylist, a makeup artist, and assorted accessories in a studio to create your best head-and-shoulder shot. A boudoir photographer can come to your home or shoot you in the studio in intimate attire for an inviting full-length look. Women will get as much of a thrill out of seeing their men in bikini underwear as men will cherish their sweethearts posing in sexy lingerie.

19. E. T. (EVERY TRAVELER) PHONE HOME

Distance makes the heart grow fonder, or yonder. It's up to you.

- 5-10 minutes each day you're away
- More than a "Hi, how are you?"
- 1-3 discreetly placed cards or gifts (optional)

Whenever you are away from your partner, at least one phone call daily is a requirement; and always try to share something intimate during each conversation. For added spice, begin the conversation with an offbeat or wild greeting using a foreign accent.

Another way to reach out and touch your loved one is to combine one or two of the calls with a little treat. Before hanging up, direct your partner to a place in the house or apartment where you've left a card or gift. For sure, you will not be forgotten in your absence.

Travel advisory: If you travel frequently, you can avoid long distance phone calls once or twice a year by surprising your partner with a ticket to join you on your trip.

20. TOKENS OF LOVE

For services to be rendered.

- Writing materials
- Knowledge of your partner's needs
- Ability to respond on cue

Present your partner with three or more coupons similar to the one shown on the next page. A coupon can be romantic or practical or just plain fun. It can be redeemed for tickets to see a favorite performer, an enchanted weekend, a full-body massage, a helping hand on demand, baking a favorite dessert, or a midnight run for junk food. One helpful hint: Be sure to offer goods and services that your partner will value, not what you might want for yourself.

Vary your coupon offers to include tasks that require immediate redemption, as well as quiet moments or events to which you can both look forward. Use the coupon offer frequently and see how quickly your popularity rises.

THIS COUPON ENTITLES

Gracie

to

George's undivided attention
during 2 hours of shopping

(Redeemable any weekend upon demand.)

THE SPICE OF LIFE

Life is a flower of which love is the honey.

~Victor Hugo

21. HOT LIPS

Whoever named it necking was a poor judge of anatomy.
~Groucho Marx

- Sweet breath
- 20-30 seconds, 3 times a day

Surprise your partner with a long hug and kiss (twenty-to-thirty seconds) that is not a part of foreplay. Just enjoy the hug and kiss for their own value. This requires no dressing up, planning, or budgeting, and the benefits are immediate.

When asked for the secret to their long-lasting marriage, a couple married for 66 years responded, "When we kiss, we kiss for a long time."

This practice has become a minimum daily requirement for our relationship; in fact, we kiss often and in many different places. We love it when strangers ask us if we just met.

For maximum results, use this recipe at least three times daily.

22. KICK THE HABIT

*Mix up the ingredients in your life
and nibble on something new.*

• Openness to change

Is your routine as a couple fairly predictable? Do you tend to favor the same restaurants, activities, and friends? If so, it's time to break out of your mold and start replacing the familiar with the unfamiliar. It's a terrific way to reawaken your partner's interest in you and the relationship and add spontaneity to your daily activities.

Do at least one new thing each week. Change your hair or clothing style or surprise your partner in the shower. Plan some activities together, like going for that ethnic food you've never tried, spending the night in a double sleeping bag in front of the fire, having a picnic dinner in bed, camping out in your backyard, or taking an exercise class together. For some open-air excitement, take a ride in a hot-air balloon, go river rafting, or rent a convertible for an evening or weekend.

23. Try It, You'll Like It

Step into your partner's shoes ∼ and walk around a bit.

- Interest in your partner's interests
- Availability
- Desire to tag along

Show how much you care by taking more of an interest in something your partner has usually done without you. Men, go shopping with your lady once or twice a month. Ladies, team up with your couch potato every now and then for Monday night football.

Sample Servings

Although I have an aversion to shopping, it is Leslie's favorite pastime. One Saturday morning I got caught up in her enthusiasm and decided to accompany her to a garage sale. While Leslie searched for her bargains, I began schmoozing with the people and helped negotiate better prices on Leslie's purchases. Now we go to garage sales on a fairly regular basis, and I get as excited as she does over great finds for our house and family.

Leslie likes going to bed early, whereas I often stay up late to read, work, or study. Although it was difficult for her at first, she decided to join me several nights a month. With the kids asleep we could talk undisturbed, read in the bath together, take a private ballroom dance lesson in our living room, eat a midnight pizza, or cuddle for an old-time movie. Actually, it was during these late hours that the manuscript for *Recipes for Romance* was born and developed.

24. Go Crazy

Love is being stupid together. ~Paul Valéry

- 1 oz. of enthusiasm
- 2 lbs. of foolishness
- Courage to break your boundaries

A little craziness mixed with a lot of playfulness may be just what your relationship needs right now. Get goofy with your partner. Feed each other an entire meal with your fingers. Have a food fight or pillow fight. Dance around the house — or do the dishes — naked. Eat a candlelit dinner in your walk-in closet. Try on each other's clothes — in the privacy of your home, of course. Go to an all-night supermarket in your pajamas and bathrobe at 2:00 A.M.; you'll fit right in with the other customers!

25. PLAY HOOKY

Take away leisure and Cupid's bow is broken. ~Ovid

- Willingness to go off the schedule
- Desire to put your partner first

Many people often complain, "I just don't have the time to be romantic." This contrasts sharply with the early days of the relationship when they first fell in love with their partners and managed to spend almost all their time together. Commitments outside the relationship are necessary and should not be ignored, but they must never replace the commitment of time and energy to one's partner — if romance is to be kept alive and well.

One of the easiest ways to break out of this rut is to schedule time with your partner when you normally wouldn't. Take a day or half-day off from work; skip a class, shopping trip, or weekly card game. Tell your partner that he or she is more important than your scheduled plans, and show you mean it by doing something both of you will enjoy.

At first you may feel a little guilty being away from the office or the gang. However, making your partner top priority can reawaken feelings of spontaneity and excitement that help keep the relationship fresh. It will also encourage you to keep each other at the top of your daily planning lists.

26. HOME ALONE, IN STYLE

Dress for sex-cess.

• Elegant attire

Pick an evening when you and your partner are going to be at home alone; however, dress up as though you were going out to paint the town. When your partner asks, "What's up? Where are you going?" answer him or her with something like, "Nowhere. I just wanted to look extra special for you tonight."

This is one of the great appetite teasers. Be prepared for the main course, and hopefully, a delectable dessert.

27. TWO-SCENTS WORTH

You'll get your money's worth even when you don't buy anything.

- 1 well-stocked perfume counter
- Clear sinuses
- Bare arms and necks

Go together to a great perfume counter and try on many fragrances until you help each other select a new perfume or cologne you both really like. You may want to purchase compatible "his and her" fragrances by the same designer; they often complement each other well. Every time you put the fragrances on, you'll remember the fun you had choosing them.

28. Mademoiselle Meets GQ

Show and tell with a sizzle!

- 1 or more intimate apparel shops
- 1 dressing room large enough for two
- 2 doses of ambition without inhibition

Ask your partner to go shopping with you for lingerie (ladies), bikini underwear (men), or a sexy silk robe or pajamas. Don't be afraid to get into the dressing room together. Even if you don't end up buying anything, you'll love the time you spent modeling for one another.

GOOD VIBRATIONS

When words leave off, music begins.

~Heinrich Heine

29. TALK OF THE TOWN

Let your partner tune into WLUV-FM
(Words of Love ~ For Me).

- 1 or more sincere, well-stated compliments
- 1 audience (your partner and at least 1 other person)

Rave about your partner in public; maybe even exaggerate a little if the urge hits you. He or she may seem embarrassed, but inwardly will be thrilled when your compliments flow to another couple at dinner, to friends at a party, or at a family gathering.

30. FOREVER YOURS

How do I love thee?
Let me count the ways.
~Elizabeth Barrett Browning

- Intimate feelings
- Writing materials
- 1 handsome frame
- 1 calligrapher (optional)
- 1 messenger (optional)

Make up a short love poem, recall a conversation from your first date together, reflect on an unforgettable time in your relationship, or develop a "Top 10" list of the things you love most about your partner. Next, record these private thoughts onto your final sheet of paper or have them transcribed by a calligrapher. Choose a frame that your partner might place in a special location. For the golden touch, have it delivered by a messenger.

31. M.V.P. (MOST VALUABLE PERSON)

"Thou shalt honor thy partner" is the first commandment of love.

- 1 custom-made trophy
- 1 thoughtful inscription
- 1 engraved object (alternative)

Order a trophy for the most valuable person in your life. Have it engraved with your partner's best qualities or endearing accomplishments. This is a gift that will keep on giving for years to come.

An alternative to this idea is to engrave a date or message on an object that has symbolic significance or sentimental value to your partner or your relationship.

Sample Serving

A sports enthusiast surprised his wife by presenting her with a two-foot-tall trophy. It is a statuette of a goddess standing victoriously on top of a Greek temple. The plaque inside the temple lists eight of her most outstanding achievements: Most Valuable Person, Best Friend, Lover of the Year, Mother of the Year, to name a few. The trophy is a continual reminder of both the early days in their relationship and their honeymoon, which ended romantically at the Parthenon in Athens.

32. FOR HE'S (SHE'S) A JOLLY GOOD FELLOW

A smorgasbord of humor and appreciation.

- 1 secret time and location
- 1 guest list
- 1 anecdote per guest
- Refreshments
- Party favors (optional)

Have a surprise party "in your partner's honor" with close friends and family. It can be done as part of a birthday or anniversary celebration, but we suggest you plan it at another time. Enhance the occasion by providing guests with party favors like hats and horns or Groucho Marx mustaches and glasses. Give each guest a couple of minutes to reveal personal and humorous anecdotes about your partner, and conclude the occasion with your own amusing story and a testimony of appreciation.

33. PILLOW TALK

I like not only to be loved, but to be told I am loved.
~George Eliot

- 1 bed
- 2 pillows
- 3 compliments
- Give and take

At night before falling asleep, comment on three things that please you about your partner. While it's easiest to compliment physical appearance, give it some thought and show additional consideration by focusing on your partner's behavior and character traits. Hopefully, he or she will want to reciprocate afterward or perhaps the next evening.

"I really appreciate the way you extended yourself to the newer employees at the office party tonight. Now the people at work know what I mean when I tell them, 'I'm the luckiest guy in the world.' " This is more meaningful than "You looked fantastic tonight."

Also, be sure to state your compliments in a positive light: "Sweetheart, you really went out of your way to help me this afternoon. I want you to know how much it means to me and I love you for it." If you say, "Thanks for helping me out today; you really shouldn't have," your partner may feel confused rather than acknowledged.

Of course, always accept a compliment graciously when you're on the receiving end. This means acknowledging the praise with a simple "Thank you," nod of appreciation, or gentle kiss. Never downplay what you are being praised for with a comment like, "Ah, it was really nothing."

Not only will the recipient of Pillow Talk go to sleep with a smile, but also it will remind you of your own good fortune. It's the perfect nightcap!

MUM'S THE WORD

Sometimes you just gotta trust

that your secret's been kept long enough.

~Anne Cameron

34. SURPRISE DATE

What a great way to whet your partner's appetite!

- 2 show tickets (or invitation to dinner)
- 1 envelope
- 1 pen
- 1-2 decorative magnets (optional)
- Ability to keep a secret

Place show tickets or an invitation to dinner or special event inside an envelope. Write a brief message on the outside of the envelope like "Surprise for my Honey," "Good things come in small packages," or "Open at your own risk. Violators will be whisked away."

Be sure to put the envelope in an area where it will be readily noticed. You may want to buy a decorative magnet like a heart, Hershey's Kiss™, or embossed photo to secure it on the refrigerator.

35. PLEASURE HUNT

A homemade amorous adventure!

- 3-5 clues
- 3-5 gifts
- 3-5 places to hide clues and gifts
- 1 mystery or romantic conclusion
- 1 strong dose of imagination

The setting can be your house, the neighborhood, or the city at large. Clues (and perhaps a few matching gifts) will guide your partner on a Pleasure Hunt from one location to another. The hunt can lead to a big mystery present, or conclude with a secret rendezvous at a romantic hideaway.

Sample Serving

I once returned from a trip to a "Welcome Home" Pleasure Hunt arranged by Jimmy. It started with a bouquet of flowers and a card on my dining room table. I was directed to my refrigerator, which was covered with magnetic Hershey's Kisses™ securing an envelope. Inside the envelope were concert tickets for the following weekend. Additional clues led me to other small gifts hidden throughout the house; the last clue invited me to Jimmy's kitchen.

I felt renewed energy as I rushed to my next destination. There, a bottle of wine and a postcard with mysterious numbers beckoned me to the master bedroom. I excitedly pushed my way upstairs through a forest of helium-filled "Welcome Home" balloons. There was a large map taped to one of the bedroom walls. It took me a few minutes to realize that the numbers on the postcard represented latitudes and longitudes; they designated vacation spots where Jimmy had made plans to take me over the next year.

Next I was invited to the bathroom, where a hot bath, candles, and my favorite music awaited me. After the bath, a final clue inside the medicine cabinet led me back to the warm bedroom. It had been transformed into a chamber of soft light and music, with pillows and blankets spread across the floor. My favorite masseur was now ready to send me to paradise with a full-body massage.

36. UNEXPECTED ANNIVERSARY

It all depends on the secret ingredient.

- 1 card
- 1 or more gifts (optional)
- 1 wild and crazy imagination

One of the big problems with birthdays, anniversaries, and holidays is that they are set dates; your loved one already expects something to happen at those times. For a nice change, plan and celebrate a birthday or anniversary on a date earlier than usual.

Also, creating unexpected anniversaries and finding unusual ways to celebrate them will add continual doses of vitality to any relationship.

Sample Serving

On one occasion while we were dating, I invited Jimmy to dinner at my house for a "sensational meal" and asked him to dress nicely for me. When he arrived, my son David met him at the door and told him he could not yet go into the kitchen. David took Jimmy into his room and entertained him as I slipped out through the back door and drove off.

Jimmy grew more curious about what was going on behind the kitchen door. After five minutes David doused him with cologne and gave him a card from me. The card invited Jimmy to find me "exactly where we were eight months earlier." David laughed as Jimmy searched desperately — first in the kitchen, then the bedroom, then throughout the house. Finally he counted back to Valentine's Day, which had been our first date together, and recalled our feast at an Italian buffet in a famous hotel by the ocean.

I felt nervous and excited as I waited for Jimmy in the lobby of that hotel. I greeted him wearing the same dress I had on eight months earlier. Tears came to both of our eyes as Jimmy rushed inside to join me.

I loved treating us to dinner, and keeping the plans secret for the week before. Jimmy still tells me it is one of the most thoughtful things anyone has ever done for him.

Remember, the odder the timing, the greater the impact. Another example can be found in recipe 37.

37. Carte Blanche

The crème de la crème of gift-giving!

- 1 card of appreciation
- 1 shopping-spree location
- As much money as you can afford

What could be more exciting than getting a generous gift certificate or "line of credit" to spend a lot of money on yourself? One thing, maybe . . . giving one to your partner.

Take your honey to a favorite store: clothing, sporting goods, electronics, antiques, crafts, furniture, jewelry, books, or sweets. As soon as you walk in, present him or her with a card of appreciation that includes a gift certificate, cash, or a credit card (if you dare!). You're going to love watching your "kid" go crazy in the candy store.

Sample Serving

Jimmy once found a novel way to present me with a much-longed-for shopping spree. One evening we picked up my son David from his karate lesson and walked to one of our favorite restaurants. As we went inside, I was amazed to see many familiar faces, balloons rising to the ceiling, and gifts piled on a table. But I was perplexed by the deluge of "Happy Birthday" greetings from family members and friends.

Jimmy informed me that this was the day I turned 39 and-a-half. It was a fun party that included crazy gifts like a cane, denture cream, and a symbolic half-liter of wine. When we returned home, Jimmy urged me to open the freezer for my birthday dessert. I told him I was too stuffed, but he insisted.

Inside the freezer was a lovely card professing his love, and it was filled with $100 bills. The icing on the cake was having Jimmy with me on subsequent shopping trips to put my newfound wealth to good use.

THE VELVET TOUCH

The saddest thing I can imagine is to get used to luxury.

~Charlie Chaplin

38. Endless Shower

The perfect way to start the day.

- 1 naked body
- 1 exotic shampoo, shower gel and loofa sponge
- 1-2 hot coffees or teas
- 2-4 breakfast pastries
- A few drops of perfume
- 2 warmed-up bath towels

Ask your partner to take a nice long, hot shower when neither one of you is rushed for time. You may want to stock it beforehand with an exotic shampoo, shower gel, and loofa sponge. Bring in coffee or tea with scones, bagels, or muffins, and await your partner with two bath towels, just heated in the dryer and sprinkled with perfume. (For even more pleasing results, combine this with recipe 40.)

39. ROMAN BATH

Let the games begin.

- 1 hour minimum to luxuriate
- 2 naked bodies
- 1 hot bath with all the trimmings
- 1 gift-wrapped bath toy or accessory
- Sea mud or clay (optional)
- 2 terrycloth bathrobes (optional)

Take a bath together and make it a memorable event with bubbles or floating candles, scented oils or soaps, a bottle of champagne, poetry, or music. Be sure to include a gift-wrapped bath toy or accessory like a massager brush or heart-shaped loofa sponge. Painting each other's face and neck with sea mud or clay adds a delightful and playful touch and accentuates the therapeutic benefits of the experience.

Allow for at least an hour to get the most out of this one. Afterward, feeling warm and relaxed, you may want to wrap yourselves up in terrycloth bathrobes and cuddle in front of a fire or in another favorite spot. We've found this to be an ideal time for soft talk and foot massages.

40. THE ROYAL TREATMENT

*With each touch, you'll make your partner
feel like a king or queen.*

- 15-30 minutes of hands-on experience
- 1 brush
- 1 massage oil or lotion
- Relaxing music
- Knowledge of which buttons to push
- Lavender scent (optional)

Spend five minutes brushing your partner's hair or giving a scalp massage. Continue with a neck, shoulder, back, and foot rub using a fragrant massage oil or lotion. Soft, soothing music playing in the background and a lavender scent in the air will enhance the relaxed mood.

A massage can precede a date, but experience shows that more often than not it leads to additional romantic follies. We suggest that it be done when neither you nor your partner is in a hurry to go anywhere soon.

41. Breakfast in Bed

This can easily turn into one of those French breakfasts:
a roll in bed with some honey!

- 1 hearty appetite
- Sensitivity to your partner's cravings
- "I'll try anything once" attitude

Make sure your partner is good and hungry, then enter the bedroom with a sumptuous meal, gourmet dish, or dessert instead of a typical breakfast. If he or she is even half-awake, you will cause quite a stir.

Sample Serving

A friend of ours surprised her boyfriend in bed one morning with an unforgettable dish. An ice bucket filled with mocha chip ice cream, drowning in a rich hot fudge sauce, was piled high with a mountain of whipped cream and topped with chocolate-covered espresso beans. Of course, she couldn't resist the opportunity to help him devour this unusual breakfast. By the time they reached the bottom of the bucket, a lot had melted all over them, so they proceeded to recipe 39.

42. I'M IN THE MOOD FOR LOVE

The four-star buffet of late-night entertainment.

- 1 uncluttered room
- Freedom from television and telephone
- Assorted flowers and candles
- 1 medley of scents or aromatherapy
- Tranquil music
- 1-2 colored light bulbs (optional)
- Special set of sheets (optional)
- Erotic accessories (optional)
- 1 dimmer switch (optional)

Set the scene for love by clearing away laundry and paperwork and turning off the television and telephone. Place fresh flowers and candles around the room of your choice. (It doesn't have to be the bedroom.) Scented candles and incense, as well as a few drops of perfume or essential oils on colored light bulbs and pillowcases, can be used in any combination to heighten the atmosphere you wish to create. If you're feeling extravagant, buy a special set of sheets just for the occasion and spray them with a scent that blends with other fragrances in the room.

Just before escorting your partner into your personal sanctuary, put on tranquil music to solidify the mood. (Soft jazz, French love songs, Enya and Gregorian chants are among our favorites.) Once inside, let the spirit of playfulness take over. You may want to experiment with erotic massage oil, Kama Sutra products, and natural aphrodisiacs like chocolate.

When you see where all this leads, you may want to add a dimmer switch to your bedroom light to create the mood more often.

COMING ATTRACTIONS

Sweet memories must be arranged for in advance.

43. DOUBLES PARTNER

Love is a game that two can play and both win.
~Eva Gabor

- 1 new activity or pursuit
- Leisure time
- Lessons (optional)
- Staying power

Develop a new hobby together: gardening, golf, tennis, bowling, piano, ethnic cooking, pottery, painting, sailing, Latin dancing, hang gliding, scuba diving, river rafting. The opportunities are endless.

Sample serving

Our good friends surprised everyone at their wedding. They took a few private lessons in ballroom dancing without telling anyone, then developed a sophisticated routine and performed it at their wedding reception to a standing ovation. The pleasure they derived from this new hobby prompted them to join a group class, which has expanded their social circle as well as their repertoire.

44. THE GOLDEN SLIPPER

Something to ease into over the years.

- A selected theme for a collection
- Regular purchases

Help your partner start a collection (stuffed animals, videos, sports memorabilia, porcelain, cookbooks) to which you can add over the months and years. It will be a good source of future gift ideas and put an end to the excuse that's heard too often, "I have no idea what to get you."

Sample Serving

Leslie has always admired blue-and-white porcelain. I am proud to have helped her acquire an extensive collection of platters, plates, teapots, vases, and decorative objects. It is the first thing most people comment on when they enter our home. I love watching Leslie describe the background of many of the pieces, including the towns and countries where we bought them. We enjoy searching for blue-and-white mementos on each of our trips.

45. THE GREAT ESCAPE

Regular gourmet treats are a necessity of life.

- Any excuse to get away
- Good sense to leave the world behind

Take a mini-vacation at least once every two months. Just get away. Waiting for the one or two weeks next year can snowball into a mountain of anxiety. You don't have to fly away to Rio or the Bahamas to relax. Take advantage of a weekend special at a local hotel or bed-and-breakfast inn; don't be afraid to request the honeymoon package. You can also visit a spa for one or two days, take a train trip, rent a houseboat or yacht, or go camping in a romantic setting.

Sample serving

Jimmy and I decided to turn a necessary business trip to San Francisco into an international getaway. We flew into the city early on the day before our meetings and checked into the Miyako Hotel in the heart of Japantown. We walked a mile to our favorite Italian bistro in Union Square for a hearty brunch. After several hours of carefree shopping, we walked back to our hotel for extended relaxation.

While I prepared a Japanese bath, Jimmy left in search of champagne and sushi. We had a Japanese picnic in bed while our immense walk-in tub continued to fill. When it was ready, we sipped our champagne throughout the prescribed Japanese bathing ritual. After a long nap, we walked to Maharani, one of the city's best Indian restaurants, where we had reserved a private alcove in the "fantasy room." We lounged on pillows for hours as the waiter brought us course after course of sumptuous dishes.

Déjà Vu

It's never too late to be young again.

46. THE GOOD OLD DAYS

Treat your partner to the milk and cookies of youth.

- Access to childhood memories
- Nostalgic props

Through your partner or friends or relatives, find something your partner loved as a child but has not experienced for a long time: Charles Chips snacks, Snyder's pretzels, Breyer's ice cream, a bedtime story or fairy tale, a whoopee cushion, an old movie or board game, a doll or action figure, a visit or conversation with a childhood friend.

Serve it à la carte or as the perfect final addition to a full-course meal.

47. LOVERS' LANE

No matter where, it's the hottest street in town.

- 1 functioning car (the older the model the better)
- 1 cassette of rock 'n roll music
- Regression to high school behavior

Relive the 50s, 60s, or 70s. Make up any reason to take your partner somewhere. Then drive to the beach or a quiet street and park the car. Pop in a cassette of vintage rock 'n roll and start necking. Be playful. Act as though you are back in high school. You'll soon discover how true it is: You are only as young as you feel.

48. NAME THAT TUNE

A piece of the American pie.

- 1 or more favorite tunes
- 2 pairs of dancing shoes
- 1 pre-arranged agreement with local band or deejay
- 1 long car ride (optional)
- Call to radio station request line (optional)

Take your partner dancing at a night club where you have arranged beforehand for the band or disc jockey to play his or her favorite song or your favorite song as a couple. Or, before taking a long ride in the car, call a local radio station that takes requests and ask the deejay to dedicate that song to the one you love.

Sample Serving

One evening I couldn't understand why Jimmy brought me to a smoke-filled bar. It definitely wasn't our kind of place. We walked to the dance floor in the back, where he introduced me to his friend Bruce, a one-man band on the keyboards. After some small talk, Jimmy coaxed me onto the dance floor. My knees weakened and I started to tremble as Bruce began the set with "Goin' Outta My Head." That song had been my number-one hit as a teenager.

As Jimmy swept me across the dance floor, I realized it was the first time I had ever danced to this song. What a perfect combination: dancing to my old-time favorite with my all-time favorite.

49. LOVE, AMERICAN STYLE
Where junk food is the preferred menu.

- 1 double feature
- 1 carload of food, pillows and blankets
- 2 pairs of pajamas (highly recommended)
- Scenic area (alternative setting)

Surprisingly, many happy couples we interviewed for this book have never been to a drive-in movie together, or haven't been to one since they started dating years ago. Just do it! And remember to bring your favorite junk food, pillows, and blankets — no kids or friends. For a real kick, go in your pajamas!

True, the drive-in has become an endangered species in some parts of the country. If you live in an area where it is now home to swap meets and flea markets, do a drive-out. Take a ride on a country or mountain road at sunset — with the food, pillows, and blankets, of course! — and stop at a scenic area. Watch and listen to the night. Let the moon and stars or the lights of the city be the feature presentation.

50. The Way We Were

God gave us memory that we might have roses in December.
~James M. Barrie

- 2 open hearts
- Knack for nostalgia

Now and then, get back in touch with those precious moments in your relationship by revisiting places and reliving events.

Sample Serving

One of our favorites is to recreate the conclusion of our first evening together. Leslie and I met on a blind date and ended up sharing a huge cinnamon roll late at night. Periodically we go back to that restaurant and sit at the same booth to eat our "nostalgic roll." And when traveling in the car late at night, we love to look for a diner where we can have a pastry together and reminisce.

P.S. THE GRASS IS ALWAYS GREENEST WHERE YOU WATER IT.

We hope the recipes in this book have served to enrich your romantic life and brought you much satisfaction. They have worked for so many couples already that we are certain they can work for you. Please feel free to send us comments on your experiences or ideas for additional recipes. They may just find their way into a sequel to this book.

Always remember: Whether you are rich or poor, famous or obscure, outgoing or shy, sought-after or forgotten, you are as capable of loving and being loved as any other person in this world. What goes around comes around, and love is no exception! So open your heart. Speak your love today!

ABOUT THE AUTHORS

Leslie and Jimmy Caplan were married on one of their romantic getaways in Istanbul, Turkey. They keep romance alive in their marriage with periodic escapades together and by following their own advice in *Recipes for Romance*. Leslie Caplan divides her time between full-time parenting and writing. Jimmy Caplan is an entrepreneur who founded and directs a successful financial public relations firm. He is a motivational speaker and former stand-up comedian, and currently teaches classes and seminars on money magnetism and negotiating. They have two children and live in Santa Barbara, California.

ACKNOWLEDGMENTS

We thank our many friends and family members whose interest and feedback helped move this book along to its destination. In particular, we are indebted to Doyle Barnett for his creative input and introduction to Marc Allen at New World Library; to our editor Becky Benenate for her unbounded enthusiasm for *Recipes for Romance* and her determination to make it the best it could be; to Kay Strom and Dan Kline of Santa Barbara Literary Service for their professional advice and encouragement; and to Rick Eisenberg for his valued long-distance support, editorial assistance, and occasional piano concertos over the phone.

NEW WORLD LIBRARY is dedicated to publishing books and cassettes that help improve the quality of our lives. If you enjoyed *Recipes for Romance,* we highly recommend the following books and cassettes:

20 Communication Tips for Couples by Doyle Barnett. This concise, accessible guide will help anyone interested in improving communication with his or her partner.

Relationships as Mirrors audio cassette by Shakti Gawain. Recorded before an enthusiastic audience of nearly 1,500 people, this audio captures one of the most inspiring speakers of our time speaking on her favorite subject: relationships.

Tantra for the West: Everyday Miracles and Other Steps for Transformation by Marc Allen. What does tantra have to do with relationships, sex, work, money, creativity, food, meditation, and freedom? Everything! In a practical, informative style, this book presents proven principles and techniques to improve the quality of your life in every one of these areas.